# Tennis for Beginning and Intermediate Players

FIFTH EDITION

## Gloria Payne
*USPTA Professional,*
*Macon Junior College Tennis Instructor*

**Kendall/Hunt**
*Publishing Company*
Dubuque, Iowa

B   403887   01

# Contents

# List of Illustrations

# *Preface*

This book is designed for use in a college physical education class. It is best used for the beginning student but can also be used for the intermediate student. I have purposely kept the information simple so that the student will not feel overwhelmed by the sport by tennis. Sequence photos of the basic strokes are included to enhance learning. A chapter on the rules and scoring of tennis is included as well as chapters on basic strategy, the vocabulary of tennis and the brief history of tennis. The tie-breaker and NO-AD scoring are explained in the Appendix.

I wish to express my gratitude to my editor, Dr. Dorothy Brown, whose help made this book possible; to Mrs. Barbara Hutto for the cover design; to photographers Ms. LeVonne Taylor and Ms. Jean Osborne, Associate Professors at Georgia College; and to graphics artist, Mr. Paul DiPasquale of Conway, South Carolina. I also wish to thank the models: Ms. Denise Saliba of Columbus College, Mr. Mark Harville of the University of Georgia, and Mr. Bob Rasile of Oglethorpe University.

This book is gratefully dedicated to my mother and to my editor.

# CHAPTER 1

# An Introduction to Tennis

In the last ten years tennis has been "booming," as both a participant and a spectator sport. Tennis has gained immense popularity as a participant sport because people have discovered that it not only is fun to play, but also provides good exercise in a short period of time. Today it is easier to have a rewarding career in tennis both as a player and as a teacher. More and more youngsters are choosing tennis over baseball, football, and other sports, a situation which means that there will be more and better players turning professional. The sport of tennis has finally lost its "country club" image and is being enjoyed by an ever-increasing number of avid fans from all walks of life.

## HISTORY

Although no one is certain where the game of tennis originated, the most popular theory is that it evolved from a handball type of game played by the ancient Greeks and Romans. By the 14th century, the game had become popular in France, where it was known as "The Sport of Kings," because it was played only by royalty. In those early days, the ball, which was stuffed with hair and wrapped in string, was hit with the open hand. The game was played indoors, a string serving as a net. Later, a short-handled paddle replaced the hand, the paddle finally evolving into the long-handled racket in use today. Leather casing replaced the string wrapping of the earlier ball, and eventually today's pressurized felt-covered ball evolved. As the game spread to other countries, play moved outdoors. In England it was played on a lawn, hence the name "lawn tennis"; a number of important tournaments, such as Wimbledon, are still played on grass. During the 1800's, Major Walter Wingfield, an Englishman, created tennis as we now know it. The introduction of the game into America is credited to Miss Mary Outerbridge, who saw tennis being played by British soldiers, while she was vacationing in Bermuda. She returned home with a racket and net. Later her brother was instrumental in forming the United States Lawn Tennis Association (USLTA), the major governing body for tennis activities in the United States. In recent years the Association's name was changed to USTA because tennis is now played on surfaces other than grass. Many important tournaments and competitions had their beginnings in the late 1800's and early 1900's, including the U.S. National Championships, Wimbledon, the Davis Cup, and the Wightman Cup. In the mid 1960's, tennis tournaments began to combine both amateurs and professionals, an action which ushered tennis into the present era.

## EQUIPMENT

The number of different kinds of tennis rackets on the market today is astounding and confusing to the player trying to make a selection. Rackets are made from a variety of materials and come in different sizes and shapes. Rackets generally fall into three categories as far as the materials from which they are made: wood, metal, and composite. Each has its own playing features, and the player must decide which best fits his style of play. Several racket sizes are also available today. These range from standard size to mid-size to over-size. The most popular choices are the mid-sized and the over-sized frames.

Selection of grip size and weight of the racket is very important in purchasing a racket. Most rackets fall into these grip sizes: 4¼, 4⅜, 4½, and 4⅝. Most female players use a 4⅜ or 4½ grip, while most male players use a 4½ or 4⅝ grip size. The grip should fit the hand with the "Goldilocks" effect— not too big and not too small. The weight of the racket is very important to performing good strokes and deserves careful consideration when one is making a purchase. Most rackets come in light and medium weights, with some odd weights such as light-heavy or light-medium. Many players have gone to the light weight because of its maneuverability and ease of swing. Again, the racket weight should be matched with the particular player. The player should purchase his racket in person so that these things can be considered, and it is helpful for him to have the guidance of a tennis professional in making the selection.

Tennis racket strings come in nylon and gut. It is not practical for the beginner or the intermediate player to use gut, which is very expensive, and these players would probably not be able to tell the difference in the playing characteristics as compared with nylon. The most important consideration when having a racket strung is the poundage or tension of the strings. The recommended tension for standard frames is 55–60 lbs., for mid-sized frames 60–70 lbs., and for over-sized frames 70–80 lbs. Generally speaking, more control is gained with higher tensions and more power is gained with lower tensions. As in the case of racket selection, it is helpful to have the guidance of a professional.

Tennis balls are much easier to purchase than rackets or strings. Balls come in two categories: pressurized and non-pressurized. The non-pressurized balls are not responsive off the racket, but they have the advantage of lasting longer. The pressurized balls, used in all tournaments and competitions, are more responsive off the racket but they wear out quickly. Beginners and intermediates frequently try to make these balls last too long. Rarely will pressurized balls last more than six sets. Because they are vacuum packed, these balls begin to lose pressure after the can is opened, whether they are used or not. Pressurized tennis balls packaged in plastic bags should be avoided because usually they are "dead," even before they are opened.

## TYPES OF COURTS

There are four main types of surfaces on which tennis is played today. The most popular surface is rubber-based asphalt, commonly called by its trade name, such as Laykold. It is a medium fast surface; gives a good, even bounce; and, because it requires very little maintenance, is a favorite of city recreational facilities, schools and colleges. Some courts, primarily in California, are built from cement. These are very fast and tend to promote the serve and volley game rather than the groundstroking game. Asphalt and cement courts are often referred to as "hard" courts. "Soft" courts are made either from synthetic clay products or from red clay. In the United States, the most common "soft" court is made from the synthetic clay and is generally found at country clubs and tennis clubs. These courts are fast-drying and require specialized maintenance, including frequent wetting with a sprinkler system. There are still some grass courts left in the United States, but they are becoming more and more rare, because maintenance is very difficult as much depends on the weather and the soil in which the grass is planted. Grass tennis courts are similar to a golf green and promote a skidding bounce of the ball. For this reason, most players will try serving and volleying more often on grass rather than staying on the baseline. Recently, a fifth type of surface has been developed: the indoor synthetic carpet, which is similar to indoor-outdoor carpet. It is a medium fast surface, but is very expensive and susceptible to tears and ripples.

## TENNIS ADMINISTRATIVE AGENCIES

The strongest and most important organization is the USTA. It has branches that function on the national, regional, state, and local levels. Counted in its membership are thousands of tennis players ranging in skill from the #1 pro in the USA to the beginner at the local level. Another powerful agency in tennis is the Association of Tennis Professionals (ATP) which controls many of the tournaments for male playing professionals. The female counterpart to the ATP is the Women's Tennis Association (WTA) which controls tournaments and activities for women pros.

## TOURNAMENT STRUCTURE

There is no longer a single tennis "season," because tournaments under the direction of the USTA are plentiful throughout the year. There are tournaments for amateurs only, tournaments for pros only, and some which mix these two. There are junior events (for those eighteen and under) and senior events (for those thirty-five and older), as well as some that are open to all age groups.

## MAJOR TOURNAMENTS AND COMPETITIONS

1. U.S. Open—The United States National Championship held at the National Tennis Center in Flushing Meadow, N.Y. (formerly in Forest Hills, N.Y.), played on hard courts
2. Wimbledon—The English National Championship held in Wimbledon, England; considered the World Championship, played on grass
3. French Open—The French National Championships held in Paris, played on red clay
4. Australian Open—The Australian National Championships held in Australia, played on grass
5. Davis Cup—team competition between men of various nations
6. Wightman Cup—team competition between women of England and the United States

## GREAT PLAYERS OF THE GAME

It is generally recognized in tennis circles that the great players are those who have won the singles championship of one or more of the tournaments which constitute the Grand Slam: the U.S. Open, the Australian Open, the French Championships and Wimbledon. To be a "Grand Slam Winner," a player must win the singles titles of all four tournaments in a single year. Only four players have achieved this distinction: Don Budge of the USA, Maureen Connolly of the USA, Rodney Laver of Australia, and Margaret Smith Court of Australia. With the Grand Slam as the measure of greatness, the greatest player in tennis history would be Rodney Laver, who won it not once but twice, once as an amateur and again as a professional. Never before had this been achieved and it is likely that it will not be duplicated. Some contemporary players deserve mention because they have won pieces of the Grand Slam and have at some time ranked #1 in the world. Foremost among this group are Jimmy Connors of the USA, Bjorn Borg of Sweden, Billie Jean King of the USA, Chris Evert Lloyd of the USA, Martina Navratilova of Czechoslovakia, John McEnroe of the USA, Ivan Lendl of Czechoslovakia and Mats Wilander of Sweden. Two rising stars of tomorrow are Boris Becker of West Germany who has already won the Wimbledon singles title and Gabriela Sabatini of Argentina.

# **2**

# The Language of Tennis

It is important for the beginning and intermediate player to be familiar with the vocabulary of tennis. Following is a list of the most common terms:

## THE COURT (Figure 1)

| | |
|---|---|
| **baseline** | the end line of the court |
| **singles sideline** | the inside sideline |
| **doubles sideline** | the outside sideline |
| **center mark** | the short slash mark that bisects the baseline |
| **alley** | the area between the singles and doubles sidelines |
| **service line** | the line in the middle of the court which runs parallel to the baseline |
| **center service line** | the line which runs under the net and connects the two service lines |
| **right service court** (also known as the **deuce court**) | the area to which each serve is made when the server is standing to the right of his center mark |

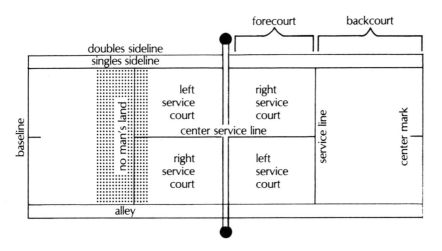

**Figure 1.** Diagram of a tennis court

| | |
|---|---|
| **left service court** (also known as the **ad court**) | the area to which each serve is made when the server is standing to the left of his center mark |
| **forecourt** | the area of the court from the service line to the net |
| **backcourt** | the area of the court from the service line to the baseline |
| **no-man's land** | the area just behind and just inside the service line where a player is apt to get balls dropping at his feet (shaded area on Figure 1) |
| **ad court** | see **left service court** |
| **deuce court** | see **right service court** |
| **band** | the canvas or vinyl tape at the top of the net |
| **center strap** | the canvas or vinyl tape at the center of the net, used to anchor the net to the ground and to keep the net at the proper height of 3 feet |

## RACKET PARTS (Figure 2)

| | |
|---|---|
| **frame** | the racket without the strings |
| **strings** | nylon or gut strands interwoven to create a hitting surface |
| **head** | the frame from the throat up plus the strings |
| **face** | the hitting surface of the strings |
| **open face** | a racket whose head is tilted backward from the on-coming ball |
| **closed face** | a racket whose head is tilted forward in the direction of the oncoming ball |

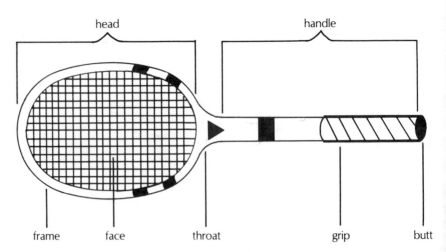

**Figure 2.** Diagram of a tennis racket

| | |
|---|---|
| **perpendicular face** | a racket whose head is straight up and down |
| **throat** | the part of the frame nearest where it expands into the head |
| **grip** | the leather part at the end of the frame |
| **handle** | the throat and grip and the area between the two |

## THE GAME, THE OFFICIALS, AND THE PLAYERS

| | |
|---|---|
| **match** | a tennis contest |
| **singles** | a tennis contest between 2 competitors |
| **doubles** | a tennis contest with 4 competitors |
| **mixed doubles** | a tennis contest with 4 competitors—a male and a female against a male and a female |
| **strategy** | the general plan for playing a match |
| **percentage tennis** | playing with the idea of cutting down on unnecessary errors |
| **rally** | the playing back and forth that takes place after the serve; also the warm-up before the match (**This action is not called "volleying."**) |
| **error** | failure to make a legal return after the racket meets the ball |
| **let** | a replay of a point or a serve because of some type of interference |
| **fault** | the failure of the server to get his first try into the service area |
| **double fault** | the failure of the server to get his second try into the service area |
| **foot fault** | illegal movement or placement of the feet during the act of serving |
| **ace** | the delivery of a serve that is so powerful or well placed that the receiver cannot touch it with his racket |
| **hold serve** | the server winning the game |
| **break serve** | the receiver winning the game |
| **approach shot** | the shot used for the transition from the backcourt to the forecourt for the purpose of volleying |
| **rush the net** | the act of going from playing in the backcourt using groundstrokes to playing in the forecourt using volleys and smashes |
| **net play** | action which takes place near the net, usually volleying and smashing |

7

| | |
|---|---|
| **net man** | a player who is positioned in the forecourt for the purpose of volleying |
| **passing shot** | the shot that goes past the net man either to his right or left |
| **poach** | the art of moving into the partner's territory for the purpose of hitting a winning volley |
| **ball boy/ball girl** | a ball retriever for a tennis match |
| **umpire** | the official in charge of the tournament match (keeps score and applies all rules) |
| **line umpire** | the official of a tournament match whose job it is to decide if balls are in or out of the boundary lines |
| **referee** | the official in charge of the tournament; in case of disputes, he is the final arbiter |

## SCORING

| | |
|---|---|
| **love** | a zero score |
| **fifteen** | the name of the first point scored |
| **thirty** | the name of the second point scored |
| **forty** | the name of the third point scored |
| **game** | the name of the point scored after forty if the score did not reach **deuce;** the name of the point scored after **ad** if the score reached **deuce** |
| **deuce** | a tie score of forty-forty |
| **ad** | the next point scored after deuce; **ad-in** refers to the server and **ad-out** refers to the receiver |
| **set** | six games won by one player who has at least a two-game lead, except when playing the tie-breaker |
| **tie-breaker** | a cut-off system to keep sets from going past a tie score of 6-6 in games; at 6-6, a series of points is played with the serving duties shared between the players and the first one to win seven points with a 2-point lead wins the set, 7-6 (See Appendix.) |
| **match** | the over-all competition, won by a female winning 2 sets and a male winning 3 sets (junior males must win 2 sets) |
| **all** or **up** | used to denote a tie score except in the case of forty-forty |
| **straight sets** | one player winning all the sets in a match |
| **split sets** | each player with one set in a three-set match or two sets in a five-set match |

8

## STROKES AND SPINS

| | |
|---|---|
| **cross-court** | a directional pattern for a stroke; moves from the hitter's right to the opponent's right or from the hitter's left to the opponent's left |
| **down-the-line** | a directional pattern for a stroke; moves from the hitter's right to the opponent's left or from the hitter's left to the opponent's right |
| **forehand drive** | the stroke used on the dominant side of the body after the ball hits the ground |
| **backhand drive** | the stroke used on the non-dominant side of the body after the ball hits the ground |
| **serve** | the stroke used to start each point, performed from either the overhead or underhand position before the ball strikes the ground |
| **volley** | a stroke used in a rally before the ball hits the ground, usually performed in the forecourt |
| **lob** | a stroke purposely hit up high, primarily to clear the net man or to gain time for re-positioning when driven out of the court area |
| **smash** (also known as the **overhead**) | the stroke used as an answer to the lob, made by coming down forcefully from the overhead position |
| **backspin** | rotation of the ball so that it spins backward as it goes toward the target, causing the ball to jump backward as it hits the ground |
| **topspin** | rotation of the ball so that it spins forward as it goes toward the target, causing the ball to jump forward as it hits the ground |
| **slice** | most often used while serving; rotation of the ball so that it spins sideways as it goes toward the target, causing the ball to jump to the side as it hits the ground |
| **flat** | little or no spin; not a good shot because it produces many errors |
| **backswing** | the initial part of the racket swing, in a backward direction to gain momentum for the swing forward to hit the ball |
| **groundstroke** | the stroke used after the ball hits the court |
| **overhead** | see **smash** |

# CHAPTER 3

# The Basic Strokes

In order to lay a foundation for fun and improvement later, beginner and intermediate players must master the three basic strokes—the forehand drive, the backhand drive, and the serve. Physical skills such as these strokes are learned through "muscle memorizing." That is, the player repeats the movements involved until the body is able to perform them with little or no conscious effort. There is a danger involved in this type of learning; bad mechanical habits can be "memorized" as easily as good ones. Therefore, it is very important that players concentrate on learning and practicing the correct techniques of the basic strokes. "Muscle memory" requires much repetition. The best type of practice for initial learning of the strokes is "air swings," in which the player performs the proper stroke through the air with his racket. This allows the player to concentrate on the arm and body movements without having to worry about making contact with the ball, with the additional advantage of his being able to practice all his strokes off the court. "Air swings" should be done several times a day for periods of five to ten minutes, preferably in front of a mirror. In order for the average player to memorize strokes, it is necessary to repeat the correct swings hundreds of times. The key to success is practicing the **correct techniques.**

## THE FOREHAND DRIVE (Figures 3-16)

The forehand drive is the groundstroke used when the ball comes to the right side of a right-hander or the left of a left-hander. The correct techniques of a forehand drive follow:

### The Ready Position

1. Stand facing the net in the "home base" position. (See Chapter 6 for correct positioning.)
2. Bend the knees slightly and place the body weight slightly forward.
3. Hold the racket at or near waist level and in the center of the body.
4. Watch the ball as it comes off the opponent's racket.

**Figure 3.** Ready position — front view      **Figure 4.** Ready position — side view

### The Forehand Grip

The Eastern forehand grip is the most efficient grip for beginners and intermediates, because it allows the wrist to be comfortable while it keeps the racket head in the proper position for the stroke. It also puts the palm in a good position to act as a brace against the force of the impact. To grip the racket correctly with the Eastern forehand grip, these steps should be followed:

1. Hold the tennis racket on **edge** with the non-gripping hand.
2. For RIGHT-HANDERS: Place the base of the knuckle of the right index finger against ridge #4 on the octagon-shaped grip.

   For LEFT-HANDERS: Place the base of the knuckle of the left index finger against ridge #1 on the octagon-shaped grip.
3. Wrap and tighten the fingers and thumb around the grip. There should be a slight gap (a finger width) between the index and third finger. The thumb should **touch** the third finger.

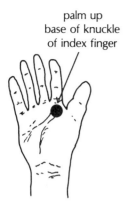

palm up
base of knuckle
of index finger

**Figure 5.** Grip guide — palm

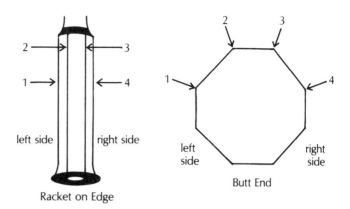

2 → ← 3

1 → ← 4

left side          right side

Racket on Edge

2      3

1                    4

left
side                    right
side

Butt End

**Figure 6.** Grip guide — ridge numbers of the grip

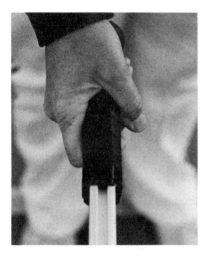

**Figure 7.** Forehand grip — front view

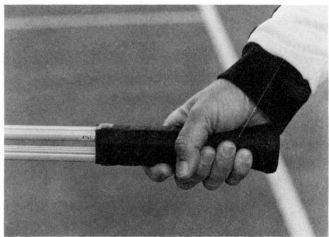

**Figure 8.** Forehand grip — side view

13

### Racket Preparation and Footwork

As the player watches the ball come off the opponent's racket and his brain signals to his muscles that the ball is coming to his forehand side, the following sequence should take place:

### Early in the Flight before the Ball Bounces

1. The shoulders and hips turn toward the forehand side.
2. The racket is drawn back until it points to the back fence, with the player using either a straight or a slightly elliptical backswing.
3. Small, skipping steps are taken to get into racket range of the bouncing ball or running steps if the ball is near the corner.

### After the Ball Bounces

4. The reaching foot (the left foot for the right-hander or right foot for the left-hander) is planted out **toward** the oncoming ball.
5. The racket begins to come forward to hit the ball, from a position slightly below the place where the impact will take place. Simultaneously, the shoulders and hips rotate toward the oncoming ball.
6. The impact takes place at the edge of the side of the body closer to the net, in line with the reaching foot and below the level of the waist at about mid-thigh (the tennis player's desired strike zone). It is very important that the player move well behind the ball bounce so that when he contacts the ball, it is on its downward arc (Fig. 15, page 16).
7. The racket follows a **straight-line path** toward the target for as long as possible, ending with a slight curve at the far end of the follow-through. The follow-through of the stroke begins at impact (Fig. 16, page 16).
8. The player returns to the ready position to await the next return by the opponent, using small, skipping steps to stay balanced.

It is extremely important that the beginner and intermediate contact the ball when it is below the waistline, so that the racket can come up through the ball with a perpendicular face. The player must learn through practice to "read" ball bounces, so that he will know when to move up or back in order to play the ball at the desired position. The wrist should be **laid back slightly and locked** just before the impact, as this insures a solid hit and allows the racket to stay in a straight line on the follow-through. The racket arm should be slightly bent at the elbow throughout the swing, so that the racket can remain in a straight line for a longer time. The player must constantly be reminded to watch the ball "like a hawk," even when his racket is making contact with it. The knees should remain slightly bent throughout the stroke, so that the player can move quickly and still maintain balance.

**Figures 9-14.**
Sequence of a
forehand drive

9

10

11

12

13

14

**Figure 15.**
Chart for
groundstroke
timing

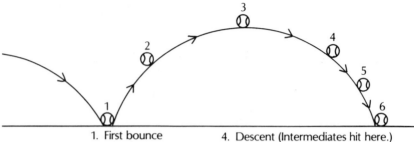

| | |
|---|---|
| 1. First bounce | 4. Descent (Intermediates hit here.) |
| 2. On the rise | 5. Descent (Beginners hit here.) |
| 3. Top of arc | 6. Second bounce |

**Figure 16.**
The shape of a
forehand swing

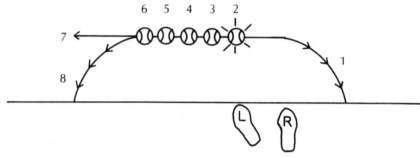

| | |
|---|---|
| 1. Backswing | 4, 5, 6. Ball remaining on strings |
| 2. Impact | 7. Ball toward target |
| 3. Beginning of follow-through | 8. End of follow-through |

## THE BACKHAND DRIVE (Figs. 17–26)

The backhand drive is the groundstroke used when the ball comes to the left side of a right-hander or to the right side of a left-hander. The correct techniques of the backhand drive follow:

### The Ready Position

The ready position for the backhand drive is the same as for the forehand drive.

### The Backhand Grip

The "light" Eastern backhand grip is recommended because it can be used effectively for both the backhand drive and the serve, thus eliminating the need for learning three grips. To grip the racket correctly, one should follow these steps:

1. Hold the racket with the Eastern forehand grip, with the non-gripping hand at the throat of the racket.

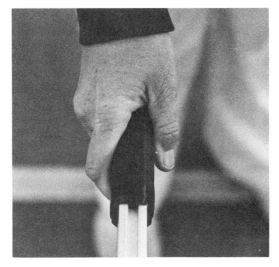

**Figure 17.** Backhand grip — front view    **Figure 18.** Backhand grip — side view

2. For RIGHT-HANDERS: Holding the racket steady with the left hand, loosen the fingers and move the base of the knuckle of the right index finger to ridge #3 on the octagon-shaped grip (Figs. 5 and 6, page 13).

   For LEFT-HANDERS: Holding the racket steady with the right hand, loosen the fingers and move the base of the knuckle of the left index finger to ridge #2 on the octagon-shaped grip (Figs. 5 and 6, page 13).

3. Wrap and tighten the fingers and thumb around the grip. There should be a finger-width gap between the index and third fingers. The thumb should be placed **diagonally** up the back side of the grip so that the **inside of the thumb at the joint** can be used as a brace to counteract the force of the impact.

### Racket Preparation and Footwork

As the player watches the ball come off the opponent's racket and his brain signals to his muscles that the ball is coming to his backhand side, the following sequence should take place:

### Early in the Flight before the Ball Bounces

1. The shoulders and hips turn toward the backhand side.

2. The racket is drawn back in a straight backswing until it points to the back fence, with the **non-gripping hand** doing most of the work; at the same time the racket is being drawn back, the grip is changed from the forehand to the backhand grip.

3. Small, skipping steps are taken to get the player into racket range of the bouncing ball or running steps if the ball is near the corner. The knees should remain slightly bent throughout the stroke.

**Figure 19.**
Chart for
groundstroke
timing

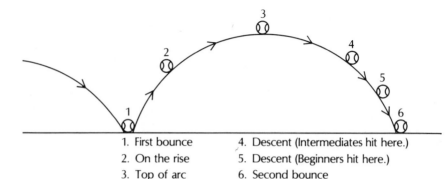

1. First bounce
2. On the rise
3. Top of arc

4. Descent (Intermediates hit here.)
5. Descent (Beginners hit here.)
6. Second bounce

**Figure 20.**
The shape of a
backhand swing

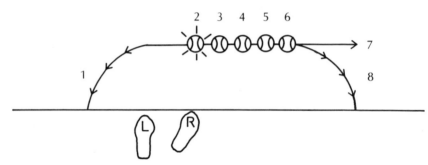

1. Backswing
2. Impact
3. Beginning of follow-through

4, 5, 6. Ball remaining on strings
7. Ball toward target
8. End of follow-through

### After the Ball Bounces

4. The reaching foot (the right foot for the right-hander or the left foot for the left-hander) is planted out toward the oncoming ball.

5. The non-gripping hand is dropped off the racket as it comes forward to hit the ball, from a position slightly below where the impact will take place.

6. The impact takes place at the edge of the side of the body closer to the net, slightly in front of the reaching foot and below the level of the waist at about mid-thigh. At impact, the shoulders and hips rotate toward the target. It is very important that the player move well behind the ball bounce so that when he contacts the ball, it is on its downward arc (Fig. 19, page 18).

7. The racket follows a **straight-line path** toward the target for as long as possible, ending with a slight curve at the far end of the follow-through. The follow-through of the stroke begins at impact (Fig. 20, page 18).

8. The player returns to the ready position to await the next return by the opponent, using small, skipping steps to recover.

**Figures 21-26.**
Sequence of a
backhand drive

21

22

23

24

25

26

Much of the success of a backhand drive depends on three major factors. First, the player must hit the backhand with the correct grip. The forehand grip is not effective for a backhand drive. Second, the player must keep the racket arm **tucked** into the ribs until mid-way in the follow-through, with the tip of the elbow pointed down at the court during the entire swing. Third, the player must keep the wrist locked during the swing to insure a solid hit.

### THE SERVE (Figs. 27–32)

The serve has one distinct advantage over all the other strokes in tennis. The server has complete control over when he will serve the ball, and if he tosses the ball up and does not want to hit it, he may allow it to drop. With all other strokes, the player is at the mercy of the opponent and must play back all the shots hit within his boundary lines or lose the point. The server must learn to take advantage of this unique aspect of the serve. He should train himself not to swing at bad tosses and not to rush either his first or second attempt.

In most cases, the serve for the beginner is simply the way to get the ball in play. Later, the serve can become a weapon to put the receiver on the defensive. Players should resist the temptation to "blast" the first serve and "powder-puff" the second serve.

### The Grip

The grip for serving is the same as for the backhand drive. If the player has trouble using this grip, he may use the forehand grip for serving. Gradually, he should work his way over to the "light" Eastern backhand grip.

### The Ready Stance

To be ready to deliver the serve, the player should follow these directions:

1. For RIGHT-HANDERS: From behind the baseline, line up the left foot and left hip with the right net post and place the right foot in a comfortable position behind the left foot. Line up the left shoulder and the eyes with the target.
   For LEFT-HANDERS: From behind the baseline, line up the right foot and right hip with the left net post and place the left foot in a comfortable position behind the right foot. Line up the right shoulder and the eyes with the target.

2. With the racket on edge, line up the top edge of the racket frame with the target, holding the racket at waist level and supporting it at the throat with the third and fourth fingers of the non-gripping hand.

3. Hold one or two balls in the non-gripping hand, touching them to the throat of the racket.

## Racket Preparation and Footwork

To serve correctly, the following sequence should take place:

1. With the weight on the back foot, the "on-edge" frame drops downward, passes by the feet and swings up toward the top of the back fence.

2. The racket head is dropped down into the "backscratching" position, so that the edge of the racket frame is near the backbone, between the shoulder blades and the small of the back.

3. With the weight now being transferred to the forward foot, the racket is extended up into the air, where it makes contact with the ball, slightly to the right of the body for right-handers or slightly to the left of the body for left-handers. A **quarter turn** of the racket frame is necessary in order to hit the ball with the strings. The shoulders and hips rotate toward the target just prior to the impact.

4. The racket face pushes the ball out toward the target and comes down in a circular path to finish past the foot which was lined up with the net post. Some players bring the back foot over into the court as a part of the follow-through. This is optional for the intermediate but not recommended for the beginner.

## Ball Toss

1. The hand holding the ball drops down in line with the front thigh for about 10 to 15 inches.

2. The hand holding the ball then reverses direction and reaches up into the air to full extension, in order to place the ball in the correct position for the hit. Correct positioning includes placing the ball high enough so that the racket can attain full extension during the hit and placing it directly in line with where the racket strings should be at impact. The ball should be placed in a position slightly forward and over to the side where the racket shoulder will pass, so that no twisting will be required to meet the ball. The player should be careful to let the fingers fall away from the ball as it is released, so that it will go straight up.

## Coordination of the Racket Swing and Ball Toss

As the racket arm begins its downward motion, the ball tossing arm drops down in line with the front thigh. As the racket arm passes by the feet and begins its swing up toward the top of the back fence, the ball tossing arm reverses direction and reaches up into full extension. The ball is released from the fully extended fingers the instant that the racket begins to go into the "backscratching" position. As the ball goes up into hitting position, the racket goes into the "backscratching" position and then extends up to hit the ball. The desired result of these actions is for the ball and racket strings to arrive in the impact area at the same instant. This precise timing takes many hours of practice, especially for beginners. It is valuable for the beginner to use these

**Figures 27-32.**
Sequence of the
serve

27

28

29

30

31

32

cue words when coordinating the racket swing and ball toss: "down together," "up together," "scratch and hit," and "finish."

It is very important for the server to remember that the racket pattern for serving is a **curved line** rather than a straight line. Too many players throw the ball in the air and hit down on it, only to drive it into the net or out of the boundary lines. The server must hit **up, out** and **over** the ball in order to clear the net and get the serve into the service area.

## PRACTICE TECHNIQUES FOR THE BASIC STROKES

Every tennis player from beginner to professional must constantly practice the basic strokes. The techniques suggested are for the beginner and the intermediate but the advanced and tournament players can benefit from them also.

1. **Air-swing.** See page 11.
2. **Ball toss drills.** One player tosses balls to the hitter.
3. **Backboard practice.** Allow the ball to bounce **at least** twice before stroking it, so that there is time to perform the correct techniques.
4. **Ball-machine drills.** A ball-tossing machine sends balls over the net to the hitter.
5. **Rally drills.** Perform on the court with a partner, with emphasis on accuracy rather than power.
6. **Serving drill.** Perform alone using a container of balls.
7. **Match play.** Play practice sets with emphasis on steadiness.

## COMMON MISTAKES AND APPROPRIATE CORRECTIONS

1. **Failure to watch the ball.**

   This mistake causes mis-hits which result in loss of control and accuracy. The player should focus on the ball as the opponent hits it and re-focus on the ball after it bounces on his side of the court. He should then watch the ball as he hits it with his racket. At the moment of impact when performing a groundstroke, the player can more easily watch the ball if he keeps his **chin down.** At the moment of impact on his own serve, the player can more easily watch the ball if he keeps his **chin up.**

2. **Late racket preparation.**

   Late racket preparation is probably the most common mistake in tennis. It is the cause of most late hits and also causes a player to leave out some important parts of the swing, such as the backswing. To eliminate this mistake from his game, the player should learn to watch the ball come off the opponent's racket and should move quickly into position to hit the ball. By the time the ball bounces on his side of the court, the player should be set up for the hit, with his racket in a good backswing position.

3. **Overhitting.**

   Tennis players on all skill levels are susceptible to the disease of overhitting—applying more force to the shot than is necessary—perhaps because they are waiting for the chance to impress the spectators and the opponent. These players fail to realize that only about *one* out of five of these "big shots" makes the point. The player should use only as much power as he can control. Control on a shot comes from a **slow,** full swing that is timed so that the ball is contacted out front, thus creating all the power a player will need.

4. **Excessive use of the wrist on groundstrokes.**

   A loose wrist or too much wrist action on the groundstrokes causes erratic hits. The best way to correct this mistake is to squeeze the grip a split second before the impact of ball and racket strings. This action will cause the wrist to lock. The squeezing action should continue until the stroke is finished.

5. **Sloppy footwork.**

   Good footwork is the foundation for good tennis strokes. It is very difficult to stroke the ball properly if the feet are out of position. Fast, short steps are best for balance and mobility. After moving into position using these fast, short steps, the player should plant the front foot out toward the oncoming ball, with that foot bearing the weight just prior to and during the impact and follow-through. In between hits, the feet should be constantly moving so that the player will be able to move quickly to the next ball. Generally, poor footwork causes the player to hit the ball at the wrong time in the ball arc. It helps for the player to move 6 to 8 feet behind where the ball will strike on his court and intently watch the ball begin to descend (Fig. 15, page 16).

6. **Circular swings.**

   Many players suffer an optical illusion when they watch good players hit groundstrokes. The swings look circular to the eye and so the beginning player goes out and swings in a circle and sprays balls everywhere. What is being missed by the eye is the **straight** line of the racket in the "impact zone" (while the ball is on the strings). Ball control will be helped by the player's imagining hitting four balls which are lined up in a row toward the target. This image should be a conscious effort until the correct stroke becomes automatic.

7. **Incomplete swings.**

   A problem frequently experienced by beginners is an incomplete swing. Many beginners think that the stroke ends with the impact of ball and strings. Actually, at the impact, the main part of the stroke is just the **beginning.** A player should think of hitting **through** the ball rather than **up to** the ball. This will cause the player to add the follow-through.

CHAPTER **4**

# The Variety Strokes

Once the basic strokes have been mastered, the player should learn to give more precise direction to these strokes, so that he can aim for specific areas of the court rather than just getting the ball somewhere within the boundary lines. The best way to give direction to strokes is by adjusting the follow-through. To hit the ball cross-court, the player pulls the follow-through across the front of the body and the ball crosses the center of the net. To hit the ball down-the-line, the player pushes the follow-through out away from the body and parallel to the sideline and the ball crosses the net near the sideline. The player can also affect the direction of strokes by adjusting the point of impact, hitting the ball earlier for a cross-court and later for a down-the-line. In either case, the racket remains in a straight line toward the target for as long as possible during the follow-through. This straight line connects two points—the impact area and the target area. The cross-court shot is the safer of the two because it goes over the lowest part of the net, and there is more court in which to hit, since the ball is traveling on the diagonal. The cross-court shot also helps the player recover to home base quicker, since the player should stand slightly off center to the cross-court side to cover the angles of return. Therefore, when the player wants steadiness, the cross-court shot is best. The down-the-line shot is useful to run the opponent and makes a good approach shot when the player wants to come into the forecourt to volley.

The intermediate player should also begin to take the ball earlier in its arc pattern, instead of allowing it to descend as the beginner does. The intermediate player should attempt to contact the ball closer to the top of its arc (Fig. 15, page 16).

The player is now ready to learn new strokes to make himself a well-rounded player.

## TOPSPIN

Putting topspin on the groundstrokes helps a player hit harder and still keep the ball in the court. It also helps the ball clear the net and can keep the opposing player pinned in the backcourt. To hit topspin, the player should

1. drop the racket head well below the impact zone so that the angle of the stroke is steeper than the regular stroke and
2. follow through in a higher path than the regular stroke.

It is very important to keep the racket face perpendicular as topspin is applied. If the racket face is open even one degree, the ball will hit beyond the baseline. Topspin can be applied using the grips described in Chapter 3 although many players adjust to more severe forms of these grips (such as the semi-Western grip for a topspin forehand).

## UNDERSPIN

Underspin is very effective when the player is rallying from the baseline, especially when performing the backhand drive. It is also effective as an approach shot because the ball with backspin tends to bounce low, thus causing the opponent to hit up to the net man. Underspin is accomplished by these techniques:

1. taking the backswing higher than usual, above the level of the on-coming ball,
2. tilting the racket head back to open the face, and
3. hitting down and out on the underneath side of the ball.

## SLICE SERVE

The serve, described in Chapter 3, is the basic topspin serve. The intermediate player should add the slice serve to his arsenal, so that he can introduce the element of surprise into his game. For the right-handed server, the slice serve will curve wide to the opponent's right in the deuce court. For the left-handed server, the slice serve will curve wide to the opponent's left in the ad court. In both cases, the opponent is drawn off the court to play the ball. The slice serve begins with the look of the topspin serve except that the ball toss is slightly more to the side. As the racket comes out of the "backscratch" position, the slice is accomplished by:

1. angling the outer edge of the racket frame toward the left net post for right-handers or toward the right net post for left-handers and
2. brushing the racket face around the outer side of the ball (an outside-in hit).

## RETURN OF SERVE

The return of serve is an important technique in the player's game. A good return of serve takes away the offensive advantage of the server and gives it to the receiver. The technique of returning will depend on the type of serve being delivered. If the server is serving hard, fast serves, the returner will use a stroke that has a shortened backswing and follow-through (a block stroke similar to a volley). If the server is serving moderate or slow serves, the returner should use the regular forehand or backhand drive. If the server is rushing the net, the returner has the option of hitting a drive as a passing shot or chipping (a shortened stroke using backspin) the ball at the server's feet.

## APPROACH SHOT

When the backcourt player moves from the baseline to the net, he must pave his way into the volley position with an approach shot, which is hit immediately before the player hits his first volley. Most players will approach the net off the opponent's short balls which hit shallow in the court or after their own serve. It is unproductive to approach the net if the player is hitting his approach shot from behind his own baseline.

A good approach shot should have the following characteristics:

1. the shot should be hit early, at the top of the bounce arc rather than on the descent;
2. the shot should be hit with underspin, the player hitting the ball **while moving** toward the net;
3. the shot should have enough depth to keep the opponent behind his baseline;
4. the shot should be hit at a moderate speed because it is not designed as a winning shot but as a set-up shot for the volley; and
5. the shot should be hit to the opponent's weakest stroke.

Once the approach shot has been hit, the player continues toward the net. As the opponent's racket makes contact with the ball, the net rusher immediately comes to a stop, using a split-step, which is accomplished by placing the feet side by side with the weight evenly distributed. This position allows the player to respond laterally to the ball hit by his opponent. If the first volley takes place before the player reaches the volley position, he should continue moving forward until reaching the desired position and then perform another split-step.

There are two tactics in placing the approach shot:

1. Down-the-line approach: player hits his approach shot down-the-line, follows the line of his shot and sets up slightly off-center to this side to cut off the possible down-the-line return by the opponent.
2. Center approach: player hits his approach shot down the middle of the court, follows the line of his shot and sets up directly in the middle of the volley position, so that the angles of the return are equal.

The player should master both of these tactics and use a mixture in his strategic plans.

## THE VOLLEY (Figs. 33-38)

This stroke is performed from the net position and is hit before the ball bounces on the court. It is designed as a way to end the point quickly. The player will usually make his way to the net under two circumstances: his opponent drawing him up inside his baseline with a short ball or the player rushing the net behind this serve. The player must be careful to approach the net behind a strong shot, one that causes his opponent to back up or run into the corner of the court. Otherwise, the net man will find himself being passed frequently.

The best volley positions for singles and doubles are shown in Figs. 48 and 50, page 44.

The correct techniques of volleying are described below:

### The Grips

The grips for the forehand and backhand volleys are the same as for the forehand and backhand groundstrokes, **if time permits a change.** Many times, the ball arrives to the net man so fast that he does not have time to change his grip. In this case, it is better to hit both volleys with the "light" Eastern backhand grip.

### Footwork Patterns

The footwork for volleying is the same as for groundstroking, **if time permits.** If not, the player should at least move his shoulders and hips around toward the impact area so that when he hits there will be some rotation.

### Racket Preparation

As the ball approaches the net man, he should follow this sequence:

1. rotate his upper torso to the side closer to the approaching ball and pull the racket as far back as his shoulder in an **abbreviated** backswing, keeping the racket head higher than the oncoming ball,
2. reach out to intercept the ball before it gets even with the body (reaching so far out front that he can see the back of the racket face when contacting the ball), and
3. block the ball with a **locked wrist,** using very little follow-through (the entire volley stroke covers only about 12 to 15 inches through the air).

The racket face should be slightly open to put underspin on the volley, and the player should swing the racket out instead of down. Swinging down on a volley will cause the ball to go into the net unless the player is very close to the net. For a low volley, the knees are bent to lower the body and the racket face is opened up more than for a higher volley. No power is applied to this shot. The most effective volleys are those which are placed out of the reach of the opponent rather than those which are "bashed" wildly.

33        34        35

**Figures 33-35.** Sequence of the forehand volley

36        37        38

**Figures 36-38.** Sequence of the backhand volley

**Figures 39-40.**
Sequence of the
forehand lob

39                    40

## THE LOB (Figs. 39-42)

The player has two choices when his opponent rushes the net. He can use the basic drives as passing shots, or he can send up a lob over the head of the opponent. A good lob has both height and depth. The height will depend on whether the lob is defensive or offensive, and depth is judged by how close the ball is to the baseline when it hits. A defensive lob is designed to drive the net rusher away from the net but can also be used to gain time for the player to recover back to position when drawn off the court to retrieve a shot. The offensive lob is designed to win the point outright and is a good shot to use against a player who gets very close to the net. Most lobs are more effective if directed to the backhand side of the opponent.

The techniques of the lob are the same as for the drives with four exceptions:

1. the backswing is not as full;
2. the speed of the racket is slower;
3. the impact takes place on the underneath side of the ball;
4. the follow-through is **up** instead of out toward the target.

Learning how to aim a lob is accomplished through practice. The player must discover exactly what angle and type of spin to use so that the ball does not land out of the court or drop too short. For a defensive lob, the angle of the racket is approximately 50 to 60 degrees; either backspin or no spin should be applied and the ball should be aimed high above the net man's racket. The angle of the racket for an offensive lob should be approximately 45 degrees. Topspin should be applied to this stroke by rolling the racket over the top of the ball during the follow-through and the ball should be lifted just barely over the racket of the net man.

30

41                              42

## THE SMASH (Overhead) (Figs. 43-46)

The smash, also called the "overhead," is the glamour stroke of tennis. It is the one to which raw power can be added, although the smash can also be a placed shot with less speed. It is the answer to a lob, especially if the lob is going to fall short in the court.

There are two kinds of smashes: ones that are hit out of the air and ones that are hit after the ball bounces. If the lob is going to come down in the forecourt or if it is not hit exceptionally high, the player should smash it out of the air. If the lob is going to come down in the backcourt or if it is hit exceptionally high, the player should smash it after the bounce. In either case, the difficult part of smashing is timing the ball flight. The hitter must watch the ball carefully, move to a position behind the place where the ball will hit the ground and move the racket up to full extension to intercept it. The racket path of the smash is similar to the serve, except that the racket is taken up past the ear to get to the "backscratching" position rather than using the sweep downward. As the ball comes to the player, he should turn his body sideways to the net and step into the smash with the foot closer to the net (the left foot for the right-hander or the right foot for the left-hander). The intermediate player should leave the "leaping overheads" to the professionals. He should keep both feet on the court while hitting this stroke. It is also unwise for the intermediate to perform backhand smashes.

**Figures 43–46.** Sequence of the smash

# CHAPTER 5

# The Rules and Scoring of Tennis

Tennis is a unique sport in that there is only one set of rules and this set applies regardless of age, sex, or locale. These rules are meant to be enforced by a chair umpire and at least ten line umpires. Playing tennis socially or competing without the help of these officials means that the players must also function as the umpire and line umpires. For this reason, it is extremely important that each player know all the rules. It is also important that each player be familiar with "The Code," a special document written for matches played without officials.

Before the match begins, the players engage in the warm-up, which usually lasts about ten minutes and is designed to limber up the muscles and strokes. All practice shots, including the serves, must be completed during this period.

After the warm-up, the players spin their rackets to decide who serves first and on which end of the court they will start.\* This spin is like a heads or tails coin toss. The winner of the toss chooses **one** of the following options and the other player or team gets the remaining choice.

1. to make the opponent choose first
2. to serve first
3. to receive first
4. to choose the end of the count.

After the toss, play begins. Tennis points follow a fairly predictable pattern, although some points are short (example: the server double faults) and some are long (example: extended rallies). Understanding the anatomy of a point can help the new player grasp the system better.

ANATOMY OF A TENNIS POINT

SERVER SERVES—RECEIVER RECEIVES
—RALLY ENSUES = POINT

Each part of the anatomy has a special set of rules. Following are the rules for singles and doubles that go with each part, plus a miscellaneous category.

---

\*The spin is done one time at the beginning of the match. From then until the end of the match, the serve alternates from player to player or team to team.

## SERVING RULES FOR SINGLES

The server must be lined up with both feet behind the baseline and within the imaginary extensions of the center mark and the singles sidelines. On the serve, the server may enter the court, if he wishes, as the ball is struck. One of the players will serve an **entire game.** The other player will take his turn in rotation. The server in the act of serving must strike the ball in the air before it bounces. The overhead, sidearm or underhand positions are all legal. The first point of **each game** is started with the server standing to the **right** of the center mark and delivering the serve into the opponent's right service court. The next point is started with the server standing to the **left** of the center mark and delivering the serve into the opponent's left service court. The next point starts to the right, the point after to the left, etc. until the end of the game. The server may allow the toss to fall without swinging at it and toss it again with no penalty. If he swings at the ball, it counts even if he misses completely. The server has a maximum of two attempts to get the serve into the proper service court. If he misses the first attempt, he takes his second. If he misses his second, the opponent receives the point. Footfaulting is not allowed while serving. There are three ways to footfault: walking or running into the serve, touching the baseline or inside the court before impact or lining up incorrectly in reference to the center mark and singles sideline. If the player footfaults on his first attempt, it is forfeited and he must take his second attempt. If the player footfaults on his second attempt, the opponent receives the point. The serve is replayed (let) if it touches the **band, center strap** or **net** before it lands in the proper service court. The serve is also replayed if it touches the above items and then hits the receiver before it hits the ground. The server must not serve the ball until the receiver is ready.

## SERVING RULES FOR DOUBLES

The size of the service courts is the same as for singles. All the rules for singles also apply to doubles except for the line up of the server and the rotation pattern. These two exceptions are:

1. The server must be lined up with both feet behind the baseline and within the imaginary extensions of the center mark and the doubles sidelines.

2. Each of the four players must serve a game in rotation. The members of the team electing to serve first decide which one of them will serve game 1. His partner will then serve game 3. After the first game is completed, the other team decides which one of them will serve game 2; then his partner will serve game 4. After the first four games of the set, the serving order is established and the players follow it, with the server of game 1 serving game 5, etc. It is illegal to break this pattern until the beginning of the next set.

34

## RECEIVING RULES FOR SINGLES

Most of the general rally rules of tennis apply to the receiver, such as getting the ball over the net, not allowing it to bounce twice, hitting it back into the proper boundary lines, etc. But there are some special rules that apply when the player is returning the serve. The receiver must let the serve bounce before he is allowed to hit it. If he hits it before it bounces, it is an automatic point for the server. The receiver may stand anywhere regardless of lines, **except** in his opponent's court. (Common sense would have the receiver standing behind the service court into which the serve is being delivered.) In case the receiver is not ready when the server serves but still makes an attempt to return the ball, he shall be considered ready. If the receiver is not ready, he should make no attempt to swing at the ball. The server must then repeat the serve.

## RECEIVING RULES FOR DOUBLES

The receiving rules for singles also apply to doubles. In addition, the following rules applies:

The receiving team makes two assignments: one of the members must receive serves in the right-hand service court (the deuce court) and the other member must receive serves in the left-hand service court (the ad court). These assignments are made independently of the serving order. The server will serve the first point to the receiver in the deuce court and the next point to the receiver in the ad court and so forth until the end of the game. This order must be maintained throughout the set. At the beginning of a new set, the receivers may change their assignments.

## RALLY RULES FOR SINGLES

After the server serves and the receiver receives, the following rules apply to the rally:

1. A player may hit the ball before it strikes on the ground or he may let it bounce one time.
2. A player must hit the ball over the net. There is one exception to this rule (see miscellaneous rules).
3. The ball must land **on** or **within** the proper boundary lines, which includes everything except the alleys.
4. The player may make contact with the ball only one time before sending it back over the net.
5. The player must allow the ball to cross over the net before striking at it.
6. The player may **follow-through** over the net as long as he does not touch the net with his body, clothing or racket.

7. The player standing inside or outside the court cannot catch a fly ball which would have hit out but **has not yet touched the ground.**

8. The player may not let the ball touch his body or anything he wears or carries **except** his racket.

9. While the ball is in play, the player may not touch the net, center strap, band, cable or net posts with his body or anything he wears or carries **including** his racket.

10. The racket must be **in** the player's hand when he strikes the ball.

11. A ball in play may bounce off the net, center strap, band, cable and singles sticks but must then rebound into the proper boundary lines.*

12. The point is played over (let) if any outside interference occurs, such as a stray ball or player from another court.


## RALLY RULES FOR DOUBLES

All the singles rally rules apply in doubles except that the alleys are in bounds. In addition, the following rules apply to doubles:

After the server serves and the receiver receives, either player may play the ball from anywhere inside or outside the court lines. Only one partner may contact the ball before sending it back over the net.

During rally, balls are allowed to bounce off the net posts but must then rebound into the proper boundary lines. The ball may also hit the net, center strap, band and cable.


## MISCELLANEOUS RULES

1. The balls and rackets must meet the standards set forth by the USTA. (Singles and doubles)

2. The umpire's decision is final unless the player decides to appeal to the referee. (Singles and doubles)

3. To even out court and weather conditions, players change ends of the court upon completing the first game of a set and following each odd numbered game thereafter. Odd numbers are determined by adding all the games played in the current set. Games from previous sets are not added. At the end of the set, if the total for that set is even (example: 6–4), the players stay on the same side to start the new set. The odd game change starts over in this set. If the previous set ends in an odd number of games (example: 6–3), the players change ends before beginning the new set and change again after the first game of the new set and every odd game thereafter. (Singles and doubles)

4. Players have 90 seconds to make the change-over described above. (Singles and doubles)

5. In junior tennis and in senior tennis, players are given an option of a ten-minute break if they split sets. (Singles and doubles)

*The net posts cannot be hit in singles.

6. A player may run around the net posts while playing the ball as long as he does not touch the posts or any part of the net and as long as he does not run into his opponent's court lines. (Singles and doubles)

7. A player may not do anything deliberately or involuntarily which hinders the opponent from playing the ball. If the act is deliberate, the opponent is awarded the point but if the act is involuntary, a let is played. (Singles and doubles)

8. If the ball in play hits another ball lying within the correct boundary lines, the player must keep the correct ball in play. (Singles and doubles)

9. The player may hit the ball outside the net posts so that it does not go over the net. As long as it does not touch any outside ground or the net posts before it lands in the correct boundary lines, his opponent must keep the ball in play. (Singles and doubles)

10. The player may reach over the net to play a ball if the ball has already hit on his side and is popping back over the net to his opponent's side. The player must make contact with the ball before it touches his opponent's court and he must not touch the net while he is playing the ball. (Singles and doubles)

11. While play is in progress, the ball may not touch fences, lights, umpire's chair, etc. If the ball does touch one of these fixtures, it is a point for the opponent. (Singles and doubles)

12. Sometimes a player will forget to switch and will serve from the incorrect side. If this mistake is discovered after any points are completed but before the end of the game, the score remains as is and the server must get on the correct side. If the mistake is discovered after the server has missed his first attempt but before he takes his second attempt, he gets on the correct side and takes only his second attempt. (Singles and doubles)

13. Sometimes a player gets confused and serves out of turn. When this happens and the mistake is discovered before the end of the game, the correct server takes over and the score remains as it is. If the incorrect server has served a fault, the correct server does not accept that fault because he is the opponent. He gets his two regular attempts when he takes over. If the game is completed before either player discovers that the wrong person served, the serving order remains altered. (Singles)

14. If the wrong partner starts serving and the mistake is discovered during the game, the correct server takes over but the score remains. If the partner has served a fault, the correct server must accept that fault and gets only his second attempt at serving. If the wrong team was serving, the other team does not accept any previous faults when the correct server takes over. If the game was completed before the discovery, the serving order remains altered. (Doubles)

15. If the receivers reverse their positions and the one assigned the deuce court receives in the ad court, they do **not** correct themselves immediately but wait until they are the receiving team two games later and then make the corrections. (Doubles)

16. If a player hits his partner while serving his first try, it is a fault and the player takes his second try. If a player hits his partner while serving his second try or while playing any other shot, the opponents receive the point. (Doubles)

## TENNIS SCORING

A. **Points make up games.**

Zero points is love.

The first point scored is fifteen.

The second point scored is thirty.

The third point scored is forty.

The fourth point scored is game unless the score has reached deuce.

Deuce is a tie score of three points each.

In the case of a deuce score, the next point after deuce is advantage or ad. If the player who has an ad wins the next point, that player wins the game. If one player has an ad and the other player wins the next point, the score goes back to deuce. The players try to score the ad point and the game point **consecutively** from deuce.

NO-AD scoring may be used instead of this system. NO-AD scoring is described in the Appendix.

B. **Games make up sets.**

A set is won by the player who **wins** six games and is at least **two** games ahead of the opponent, except in the case of the tie-breaker (see Appendix).

C. **Sets make up the match.**

Players in female events including mixed doubles and players in junior and senior events must win **two sets** to win the match. Males playing in open events must win **three sets** to win the match unless otherwise specified by the tournament committee.

### How to Read Tennis Scores in the Newspaper

The set scores are written down in sequence, with the winner's scores coming first followed by the loser's scores.

**Examples:**

Evert-Lloyd defeated Austin 6–2, 6–3
Navratilova defeated Sabatini 1–6, 7–5, 6–4
McEnroe defeated Connors 6–2, 6–3, 6–1
Borg defeated Lendl 4–6, 6–3, 6–2, 6–2
Wilander defeated Becker 6–2, 3–6, 6–4, 1–6, 6–2

# TENNIS ETIQUETTE

Tennis etiquette is based on good sportsmanship and tradition. Players must learn to be competitive but fair to their opponents. Because social players and many tournament players must play their matches with no officials, they must learn to apply the tennis rules themselves in a fair and sportsmanlike manner. The following items should be used as a guide to this task.

1. Any ball which cannot be called out **with certainty** is good. Each player is responsible for making calls on all balls landing on his side of the court. All calls of "out" should be made clearly and **instantly.** If a player knows that his partner made a bad call, the player should overrule him.

2. Players should refrain from using abusive language or engaging in equipment abuse such as throwing rackets or bashing balls. In many tournaments, the point-penalty system takes care of this type of behavior.

3. The score should be called aloud after each point is scored. Any player may do this although traditionally the server performs the task. When the score is called out, the server's score is called first.

4. The server should have 2 balls at the start of **each** point.

5. The receiver should not hit an out-of-bounds first serve.

6. When the occasion dictates, a player should say "good shot" to his opponent.

7. Each player should pick up his share of stray balls. When balls from other courts come into a player's court, they should be returned in a polite manner, but **not** while a rally is in progress. Players should not run into another court to pick up a stray ball if a rally is in progress.

8. During the warm-up, the player should hit the balls **to** the opponent rather than **away** from him.

9. The players should wear proper tennis attire.

10. As spectators, the fans should remain quiet while the ball is in play and clap and cheer only after the point is completed. Fans should never become involved in line calling or any other officiating duties.

# CHAPTER 6

# Tennis Strategy: Singles and Doubles

There is more to tennis than the ability to execute strokes properly. The good player knows where to hit the ball and how hard to hit it. Playing ability must be combined with court strategy.

## BEGINNER'S STRATEGY FOR SINGLES AND DOUBLES

The beginner has so much to worry about that strategy is relatively unimportant to him. However, there are two plans of strategy which beginners should keep in mind when practicing and playing matches.

1. Get the ball over the net. This plan applies to every level of player from the beginner to the best player in the game. Hitting the ball into the net is total failure. There is no hope for the shot if it does not clear the net. It is surprising how many tennis players completely ignore this fact. The player should regard the net as a wall and must make every effort to get the ball over it.

2. Be consistent in playing balls in the boundary lines. Beginners need to remind themselves that tennis is a game of errors and the player who makes the least number of errors will win in most cases. Learning the game is more fun for beginners if they will attempt to play as many balls over the net and in the court as possible rather than as few as they can. The beginner who "slugs" the ball in a wild manner is not a good partner. Most of the time is spent chasing his wild hits and very little time is spent in rallies. Power has **no** place in the beginner's game and plays only a limited role in the intermediate's game. Players on these levels should be defensive players, playing as many balls as possible before missing. The player should be reminded that one of the major keys to ball control is watching the ball at all times.

## INTERMEDIATE STRATEGY FOR SINGLES AND DOUBLES

Intermediate players need to continue to concentrate on getting the ball over the net and into the boundary lines. Gradually, as skill becomes greater, the intermediate can incorporate the following strategies into his game:

1. Add controlled power to all strokes. Wild, hard shots are no good if they go out. Power is best added very slowly. It is a great temptation for the player to watch the professional on T.V. and try to hit with the same speed. This quickly adds up to frustration.

2. Blend offensive tennis with defensive tennis. Whether the player will be primarily a defensive player or an offensive player will depend to a great degree on his basic personality. The offensive player—the serve and volley player—usually has an agressive personality and is a bit short on patience. The defensive player—the groundstroker—is usually long on patience and is willing to keep the ball in play until his opponent makes the error. As in other sports, a blend of these two is the winning combination.

3. Rally cross-court. Most of the groundstroke rallies should go cross-court because the net is lower in the middle than on the sides and since the ball is traveling on the diagonal, there is more court in which to hit.

4. Play to the opponent's weakness, especially on important points. The warm-up is a good time to discover the opponent's weaknesses.

5. Make the opponent hit the ball on the run. Since it is much easier to hit the ball while standing still, hitting on the run will produce a higher percentage of errors. The two best ways of making an opponent run are (a) hitting the ball corner to corner and (b) using the drop shot-lob pattern to run the player up to the net and back to the baseline.

6. Learn to vary the speed and spin of the ball. A constant diet of one kind of shot gives the opponent the advantage because he knows what to expect. A tennis player with only one speed and spin is like a baseball pitcher with only one pitch.

7. Try to achieve depth on the groundstrokes. The player should aim for the area of the court near the baseline. This depth keeps the opponent from taking advantage of the short ball. The best way to accomplish depth is to hit the ball higher over the net. The player should hit most groundstrokes 3 or 4 feet over the top of the net unless his opponent is in the net position, in which case the passing shot should come low over the net.

8. Maintain good "home base" positioning (Figs. 47–54, pages 44–45). In singles, when groundstroking from the backcourt, the player should, after each stroke, place himself a few feet behind the baseline and slightly off center to cut off the possible cross-court return (Fig. 47). In singles, when volleying from the forecourt, the player should follow the line of his approach shot so that he is slightly off center to cut off the possible down-the-line passing shot (Fig. 48). In doubles, the "home base" is approximately in the center of the area each partner is assigned to protect and a few feet behind the baseline when the players are groundstroking (Fig. 49). The net position in doubles is near the center of the area each partner is assigned to protect and a few feet away from the net (Fig. 50). In doubles, the player's first responsibility is protecting his own alley. When serving in singles, the player should be near the center mark, so that he can protect his entire court (Fig. 51). For service in doubles, the best position is near the singles sideline, so that the player can protect his alley (Fig. 52). Good positioning when receiving the serve depends on the ability of the server and the types of serves he is using. Generally, the harder the opponent serves, the farther back the receiver should stand to receive, usually behind the baseline (Fig. 53). If the opponent has a very soft serve that just barely clears the net or a twisting serve that breaks sharply to the left or right, the receiver should stand inside the baseline (Fig. 54).

**Figures 47–54.**
Home base
positioning
(R = right
position; L = left
position)

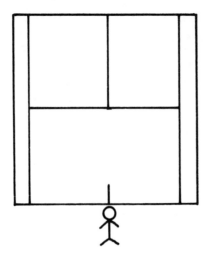

**Figure 47.** Groundstroking – singles

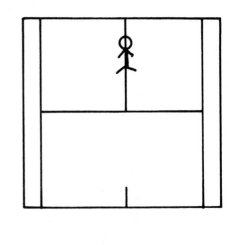

**Figure 48.** Volleying – singles

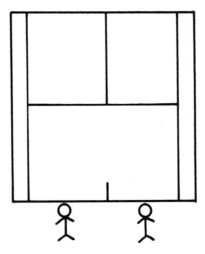

**Figure 49.** Groundstroking – doubles

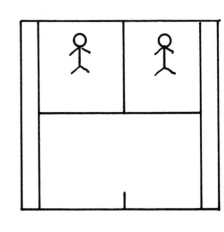

**Figure 50.** Volleying – doubles

44

**Figure 47–54.**
*Continued*

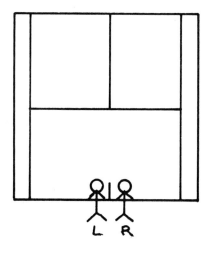

**Figure 51.** Serving positions – singles

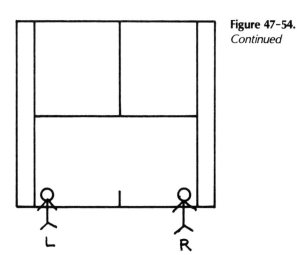

**Figure 52.** Serving positions – doubles

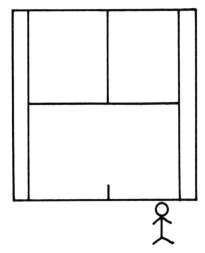

**Figure 53.** Receiving position – hard serves

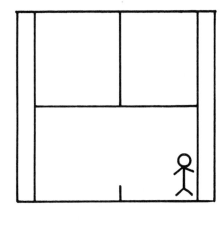

**Figure 54.** Receiving positions – soft serves

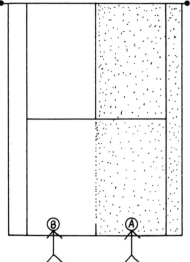

**Figure 55.** Coverage responsibilities in doubles (player A covers shaded area; player B covers unshaded area)

**Figure 56.** Common serving position in doubles (1 = server; 2 = server's partner)

## SPECIAL STRATEGY FOR DOUBLES (Figs. 55–60)

1. Teamwork is extremely important in doubles. Each partner should assume responsibility for covering his assigned territory (Fig. 55, page 46), but should be alert to assist his partner when necessary.

2. Partners should give moral support to each other. It is easy to get angry at the partner for missing a shot, but anger usually makes him play worse rather than better. It is important for the partners to communicate with each other, with plans of strategy and commands of "yours" or "mine."

3. Partners should remain side by side as much as possible. Playing parallel helps the partners keep the court covered and cuts down on the possibilities of opponents taking advantage of gaping holes.

4. The net position is the desirable one in doubles. Usually, the server's partner is posted at the net and the server comes up to join him as soon as possible (Fig. 56, page 46). The receiving team has two options: both players back, moving into the net together at the first opportunity, or one player back and his partner half-way up, then moving into the net together if the receiver hits a good, strong return or the front man joining his partner in the back if the return is weak (Figs. 57–58, page 47).

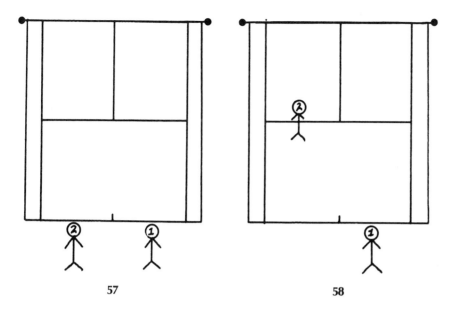

**Figures 57-58.**
Common
receiving positions
in doubles
(1 = receiver;
2 = receiver's
partner)

57

58

5. When both partners are at the net, they should shift **slightly** toward the side of the opponents' court to which they just hit the ball. This shift helps protect the alley and the middle of the court and leaves the opponents with the choice of a sharply angled cross-court shot or a lob (Figs. 59–60, page 48).

6. It is very important in doubles for the server to get his first serve into the court. This serve should be a medium paced serve to give the server time to get to the net behind it and it should frequently be placed to the backhand sides of the opponents. Because a server's first serve is usually stronger than his second, getting the first serve in applies extra pressure to the opponents in three ways:

    a. It forces the receiver to return the server's best serve.

    b. It gives the server's partner (the net man) a better chance to volley a weak return.

    c. It gives the server a better chance to come up into the volley position.

7. When returning the serve in doubles, the player will find that the best return is a cross-court shot to the back man or a chip at his feet if he is coming into the net. Occasionally, the receiver should lob over the net man on return of serve.

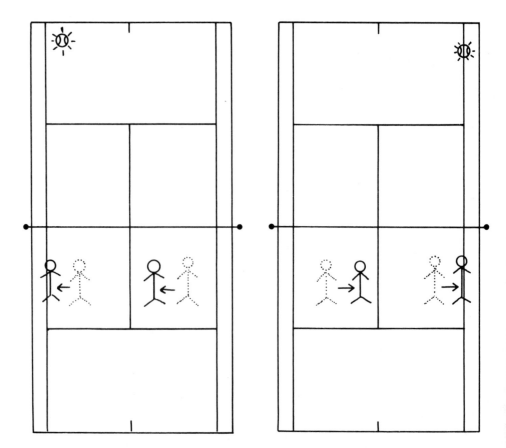

**Figure 59.** Position shift to the left in doubles

**Figure 60.** Position shift to the right in doubles

8. If both players are at the net when the opponent lobs, it is easier for the player over whom the ball passes to turn around and chase the ball. If one player is still in the backcourt when the lob goes over the net man, it is easier for him to cross behind his partner and chase the ball. When this happens, the net man should cross over into his partner's territory, staying at the net if his partner hits a good return.

9. If there is a weaker opponent, most critical points should be played to him.

10. If there is no obvious opening to play into, the player should frequently elect to hit the ball down the middle between the opponents. That middle area is sometimes weak because each partner thinks the other is going for the ball. It is not unusual to see neither player make a move to hit the ball in this situation. It is also wise occasionally to play the ball down the alley of the net man, especially if the net man tends to move toward the center of the court.

# Appendix
# *Playing the Tie-Breaker,*
# *NO-AD Scoring*

## PLAYING THE TIE-BREAKER

Almost every tournament now uses some form of a tie-breaker. NCAA college events and sanctioned tournaments use the 12-point tie-breaker. Using the power given to them by the USTA, some tournament committees declare that the last set (the third set of a three-set match and the fifth set of a five-set match) will be played to its completion without the use of the tie-breaker.

The 12-point tie-breaker is explained below.

The 12-point tie-breaker starts at 6 games apiece. The player whose turn it is to serve will start the tie-breaker. The first player or team to win 7 points wins the tie-breaker IF that player or team has at least a 2-point lead. When one player or team has won 7 points but leads by only 1 point, play must continue until someone leads by 2 points. This completes the set 7–6. The score is called 1, 2, 3, 4, 5, 6, and 7 instead of fifteen, thirty, etc.. Players change ends of the court after 6 points and any multiples of 6 thereafter. After the tie-breaker is completed, the players change ends of the court and are allowed the 90-second rest. The player or team who RECEIVED FIRST in the tie-breaker will SERVE FIRST in the next set. In doubles, the serving order pattern for that set is preserved in the tie-breaker, with each player serving when it is his turn.

## SAMPLE CHART SHOWING SERVING ORDER*

PLAYER A (A): serves point #1 into the deuce court
PLAYER B (B): serves point #2 into the ad court
               serves point #3 into the deuce court
PLAYER A (C): serves point #4 into the ad court
               serves point #5 into the deuce court
PLAYER B (D): serves point #6 into the ad court
               PLAYERS CHANGE ENDS OF COURT.
               serves point #7 into the deuce court
PLAYER A (A): serves point #8 into the ad court
               serves point #9 into the deuce court
PLAYER B (B): serves point #10 into the ad court
               serves point #11 into the deuce court

*Doubles order is in parentheses.

PLAYER A (C): serves point #12 into the ad court
PLAYERS CHANGE ENDS OF COURT.
serves point #13 into the deuce court
PLAYER B (D): ETC. UNTIL ONE PLAYER OR TEAM WINS 7
POINTS AND IS AT LEAST 2 POINTS AHEAD.

## NO-AD SCORING

There is an alternative scoring method for winning a game. NO-AD scoring can replace the traditional 15, 30, 40 method. The actual playing of the point is the same in both methods. When using NO-AD scoring, the players call the points, 1, 2, 3 and 4. A game is won when a player or team wins 4 points. If the score reaches 3–3, the player or team does not have to win two more points—there is **no "deuce–ad" situation.** At 3–3, the receiver tells the server into which service court the serve must be served. Below is a comparison chart of the two methods.

| In traditional scoring, if the score is: | In NO-AD scoring, the score would be: |
|---|---|
| 15–love or love–15 | 1–0 or 0–1 |
| 15–15 | 1–1 |
| 30–love or love–30 | 2–0 or 0–2 |
| 40–love or love–40 | 3–0 or 0–3 |
| 30–15 or 15–30 | 2–1 or 1–2 |
| 30–30 | 2–2 |
| 40–15 or 15–40 | 3–1 or 1–3 |
| 40–30 or 30–40 | 3–2 or 2–3 |
| Deuce | 3–3 |
| Ad | Game |

# Bibliography

Cummings, Parke. **American Tennis: The Story of the Game.** Boston: Little, Brown and Company, 1957.

Powel, N. E. "The Code." Princeton, N.J.: United States Tennis Association, 1974.

United States Tennis Association. **USTA Yearbook and Tennis Guide 1978.** Lynn, Mass.: H. O. Zimman Inc., 1978.